# STARTER
# LEGENDS

# Ohia and
# the Animals

## Macdonald Educational

Once there was a man
called Ohia.
He lived in Africa.

Ohia and his wife were sad.
They had no children
and no money.
They never had any luck.

3

One day, Ohia thought of a way
to earn some money.
He decided to make some palm wine.
He needed sap from the trees.

4

Ohia went to see a rich farmer.
He said "May I cut down
some of your trees?
I want to use the sap for palm wine."

Ohia spent all day
chopping down trees.
In the evening,
he put down bowls to collect the sap.

6

Next morning,
Ohia went back to collect the sap.
But someone had stolen it all.
Ohia's bowls were broken.

Ohia was very sad.
But he cut down some more trees.
In the evening,
he put out some more bowls.
Ohia hid and waited for the thief.

The thief came
in the middle of the night.
Ohia jumped out to catch him.
He saw that the thief was a deer!

9

The deer ran off into the forest.
Ohia ran after him. They ran
until they reached the court
of the king of the animals.

10

The deer went up to the king.
"Help me! This man is chasing me!" he said.
Ohia shouted:
"The deer stole my palm sap!"

The animal king was sorry for Ohia.
"The deer was wrong to steal," he said.
"To make up for it,
I will let you understand our animal language."

12

The king told Ohia not to tell anyone
he could understand animals.
If he did, Ohia would die.
Ohia went home sadly.
He did not see how this would help him.

But after a while,
Ohia and his wife began to have good luck.
They made plenty of palm wine.
Ohia's wife sold it at the market.

14

Now Ohia and his wife were happy.
They had a baby son.
They were not rich,
but they had enough money.

15

One day, Ohia was swimming
in a pool near his house.
He heard two hens talking. One said:
"Guess what? I found some gold
buried in that man's garden."

Ohia dug up his garden.
He found a huge pot of gold.
Now he was a very rich man.

Ohia built himself a new house.
He bought new clothes.

18

Men were allowed many wives where Ohia lived.
Now Ohia was rich he married a new wife.
She was young and beautiful.

Ohia's new wife did not like his old wife.
She thought the old wife and Ohia
were always laughing at her.
She often cried.

20

One day, Ohia was sitting in the garden.
He heard two mice talking.
They were planning to steal food
from Ohia's kitchen.

Ohia thought the mice were funny.
He started to laugh at them.
"There you go again," said the young wife.
"You are laughing at me!"

22

"No I'm not!" said Ohia.
But he could not tell her why he laughed.
The wife went to the village chief.

She made such a fuss
that the chief sent for Ohia.
"Tell her why you laughed," the chief said.
"Or she will make us all miserable."

24

Ohia did not know what to do.
He knew he would die
if he told them the secret.
But he was so tired of keeping the secret.

So Ohia said:
"All right. I will tell you.
Then I will have to die."

26

Ohia told everyone he could understand
the language of animals.
He told them about the hens.
He told them about the mice.
Then, sadly, he went home to die.

# Index

 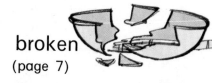